A MARKETER'S GUIDE TO HIPAA

RESOURCES FOR CREATING EFFECTIVE AND COMPLIANT MARKETING

KATE BORTEN, CISSP, CISM
FOREWORD BY CHRIS HOUCHENS

a division of

A Marketer's Guide to HIPAA: Resources for Creating Effective and Compliant Marketing is published by HCPro, Inc.

Copyright 2006 HCPro, Inc.

All rights reserved. Printed in the United States of America.   5   4   3   2   1

ISBN 1-57839-875-4

HCPro, Inc., provides information resources for the healthcare industry.

HCPro, Inc., is not affiliated in any way with the Joint Commission on Accreditation of Healthcare Organizations, which owns the JCAHO trademark.

Chris Houchens, Reviewer
John Gettings, Editor
Richard L. Johnson, MA, Senior Managing Editor
Matthew Cann, Group Publisher
Doug Ponte, Cover Designer
Jackie Diehl Singer, Graphic Artist

Jean St. Pierre, Director of Operations
Darren Kelly, Production Coordinator
Phyllis Lindsay, Copyeditor
Sada Preisch, Proofreader
Paul Singer, Layout Artist

Advice given is general. Readers should consult professional counsel for specific legal, ethical, or clinical questions.

Arrangements can be made for quantity discounts. For more information, contact

HCPro, Inc.
P.O. Box 1168
Marblehead, MA 01945
Telephone: 800/650-6787 or 781/639-1872
Fax: 781/639-2982
E-mail: customerservice@hcpro.com

Visit HCPro at its World Wide Web sites:
www.healthleadersmedia.com, www.hcpro.com and *www.hcmarketplace.com*

9/2006
20953

Contents

About the authors

Kate Borten, CISSP, CISM, is president of The Marblehead Group, Inc., in Marblehead, MA. Borten provides her clients an unparalleled blend of technical and management expertise, information security knowledge, and the insider's understanding of the world of healthcare. She is a nationally recognized expert and frequent speaker on the topics of HIPAA and health information privacy and security. She is also the author of *Guide to HIPAA Security Risk Analysis* (HCPro, 2004) and *HIPAA Security Made Simple* (HCPro, 2003), a contributor to newsletters on HIPAA privacy and security, and three-year chair of HealthSec, the premiere annual conference on information security in healthcare.

Chris Houchens is a marketing speaker, writer, blogger, and the owner of Shotgun Concepts, a marketing firm he founded in 1997 to provide marketing guidance to today's forward thinking companies. He has an extensive background in both media and marketing. Chris has a consulting specialization in the healthcare industry with clients ranging from pharmacies to medical practices. Houchens, with his company, Shotgun Concepts *(www.shotgunconcepts.com)*, was recognized as one of the nation's most remarkable marketing resources in Seth Godin's Bullmarket Directory. Chris is a well-known speaker with several keynotes and presentations dealing with healthcare and other marketing topics. Houchens is a contributing writer and source for numerous online resources and print publications. Chris' blog, the Shotgun Marketing Blog, has been cited as a marketing blog to watch and is read daily by hundreds of subscribers. Visit it at *http://shotgunconcepts.blogspot.com.*

Foreword

The Health Insurance Portability and Accountability Act (HIPAA) of 1996 has changed many things in the healthcare world. But HIPAA has not changed the fact that, in order to be competitive and successful in the market, healthcare providers must be proactive in their marketing. They must constantly search for new patients and maintain open communication with present ones.

The need to be proactive in marketing healthcare services comes down to one word: choices. In the past, when there were only one or two choices of action on a healthcare problem, whatever a doctor suggested was usually done. To a large extent, that is no longer the case today.

The amount of information available to patients increases every day. Double-checking the judgment of healthcare providers no longer stops at the "second opinion." The Internet has made it possible for patients to have a world of medical knowledge at their fingertips, some of it legitimate and some of it not. Medical marketers have to remember that the competition is not just other doctors. The rise in popularity of alternative medicine, herbal treatments, and other forms of self-diagnosis makes the entire world the competition.

Patients are more active than ever before in the decisions involving their healthcare. They have more disposable income, and limited insurance options now mean that the patient shops for medical care. The healthcare decision is more akin to a purchase than a treatment option. Just as a person might be influenced in the purchase of a new car by a postcard from the dealership, a television commercial, recommendations from friends, and researching cars on the Web, those same things influence that person when he or she is making a healthcare purchase.

Healthcare practitioners must stop thinking of the person standing across from them as a "patient" and start thinking of that person as a "customer." A customer who has choices: to participate in the treatment, go across the street to another healthcare provider, find alternative treatments, or not be treated at all. Marketing will influence the decision that customer makes.

The healthcare industry must see itself as one of many choices available to consumers. Successful healthcare marketing must not only stand out from other healthcare options, but must also rise above the other clutter and distractions that the public deals with daily.

But it wasn't always this way. In fact, the idea of marketing healthcare services is a fairly recent development. Look at the history of how healthcare has been marketed to fully understand the effect that HIPAA is currently having on healthcare marketing.

Healthcare marketing in a world without HIPAA

In the not-so-distant past, marketing in the medical and healthcare fields was either an extreme soft sell or nonexistent. Doctors and other healthcare practitioners held themselves to a level of "professionalism" that would not allow them to "sell" their services. If a doctor did happen to do any advertising or marketing, it was text-based, with only the basic contact information and no call to action.

In 1975, the Federal Trade Commission (FTC) filed an antitrust suit against the American Medical Association (AMA) concerning its code of ethics. The AMA code of ethics was the "professional code" that forbade physician members from advertising. The FTC argued that the restrictions discouraged competition and unfairly disadvantaged consumers. The FTC prevailed in the suit in 1982, and the AMA changed the code to allow advertising and other types of marketing.

Still, most physicians and healthcare providers did not immediately begin advertising. The stigma of being a "medical hawker" among one's peers still kept most established practitioners from marketing. And even though marketing and soliciting business was now ethically acceptable, most healthcare providers didn't bother. High insurance and government reimbursements meant profits even with low patient traffic. More important, the public was well trained in the process:

1. I'm sick.

2. I'll go to the doctor.

3. He'll look at me and give me a prescription.

4. I'll go to the pharmacist.

5. Repeat as necessary.

Then things changed.

Reimbursements started to shrink. Patients started to realize there were two (or more) doctors in town who could take care of their problem; there were alternative medicines and treatments that could help them; medication could be received through the mail. In general, the public realized they had choices and became more involved in the healthcare decision process.

The need to market oneself or one's healthcare facility became apparent. Also as a new generation of medical practitioners began their practices in the 1980s and 1990s, they did not have the specter of the old ethical codes stopping them (mentally) from marketing. Healthcare marketing became more prevalent and accepted both in the industry and by the public.

In addition to the core healthcare industry starting to communicate with the public, other healthcare entities' approach to marketing changed as well. Laws dealing with industries such as pharmaceuticals and insurance became more lax. These and other sectors began marketing their healthcare offerings directly to the public, bypassing the traditional doctor-patient model.

Realizing that they were no longer an exclusive choice, hospitals, doctors, and other medical providers began marketing their standard procedures and started to offer more elective procedures. In some cases, they used the hard-sell approach and appealed directly to the consumer. In other cases, they offered something more like an educational and community health model in order to demonstrate their expertise and offerings.

Healthcare practitioners welcome direct marketing

Of course, some of this marketing took the shape of traditional mass media, printed materials, and personal sales. But healthcare practitioners also discovered the power of direct marketing. They could direct a specific marketing message to specific, pretargeted patients in their office's medical database.

A healthcare database is vastly superior to the databases in the rest of the marketing world. Whereas a customer might be hesitant to provide sensitive demographic data to a store or other retail/service outlet, he or she gladly fills out medical forms, complete with their most sensitive private information. In addition, this data is certified correct on a regular basis, as patients come in for new visits and update their profiles. Add to this recent technological advances such as electronic billing and new electronic medical records (EMR) systems that create a combined customer relationship management (CRM) database and system that is unmatched in accuracy and depth of data.

Healthcare marketers could see how often patients come in, what diagnosis was made, how much they spent, whether it was private pay or insurance, and a multitude of other queries that could be pulled from the database. These slices of information could be combined and cross-tabulated to produce an extremely targeted pool of patients to make offers to about products and services, to educate and inform, or to create other relevant targeted communications. The database was a golden tool.

And then came HIPAA.

HIPAA's Privacy Rule redefines marketing

Congress passed HIPAA in 1996, with different sections becoming active in the early part of the 21st century. While the Act's original purpose was to change the way providers, patients, and the government handle insurance, one section of HIPAA, the Privacy Rule, has seemed to overshadow the others.

Healthcare providers had to start providing and posting their Privacy Policy. Patient flow and medical office logistics had to be changed to protect patients' privacy. There were now extra steps in patient registration to sign up patients who wanted to be included in marketing communications. And that fabulously accurate database now became a list of people who could potentially trigger a complaint that could lead to fines.

And now, the healthcare industry finds itself at a similar crossroads to the one it found itself at after the FTC lawsuit. The government has redefined the way that healthcare can be marketed to patients. And just as in the early 1980s, healthcare practitioners have dealt with that fact in different ways.

Healthcare marketers typically have dealt with HIPAA in one of three ways. Some entities kept doing what they had always been doing and took the risk of triggering complaints. Most attempted to follow the rules, even though they may not have fully understood them. And some healthcare providers stopped using their databases for marketing.

Healthcare entities should not be afraid to use patient data in marketing. HIPAA does not outlaw the use of medical databases. It merely sets forth guidelines and procedures for making sure that the private, personal information a person provides for his or her medical care is not used in improper ways. This is good for the patient.

It's good for the marketer, too. While database marketing is effective, there still are people who don't wish to be on the receiving end of direct marketing. This is evident in the response to initiatives such as the state and federal do-not-call lists, do-not-mail lists, and opt-outs for electronic or e-marketing. Not wasting resources and attention on recipients who have identified themselves as poor prospects increases the effectiveness and overall ROI of a marketing campaign. The sections of HIPAA that deal with marketing help identify patients who want to be left alone. This helps ensure that the marketing communications that are sent will be well received by qualified prospects.

Add to this the fact that although database marketing is effective, it's not the only marketing tool available. There are numerous nondatabase options that are extremely effective in reaching narrowly defined target markets and communities. If HIPAA prevents a certain type of communication, there is always another way to get the message out.

This book should remove some of the fear about HIPAA and marketing and clarify gray areas that are currently often misunderstood. In addition, it gives a great snapshot and summation of what HIPAA does and how it influences healthcare. And finally, it will provide some marketing ideas for working with HIPAA, working around HIPAA, and working without HIPAA.

Healthcare marketing cannot be abandoned. HIPAA is here and is not going away. Healthcare marketers must learn to deal with the situation and be proactive in communicating with their patients.

—Chris Houchens
    June 2006

HIPAA basics

HIPAA basics

The Health Insurance Portability and Accountability Act (HIPAA) passed by Congress in 1996 was initially intended, as the title suggests, to accomplish two things:

1. Ensure greater portability of a person's health insurance coverage when leaving a job

2. Provide stronger accountability tools for the government

However, Congress also attempted to reduce the high cost of healthcare by adding the Administrative Simplification section to the law, a step that has had far greater impact on the industry and patients across the country than either portability or accountability.

Administrative Simplification

Administrative Simplification recognizes that healthcare providers and payers increasingly exchange information electronically, and that if the exchanges or transactions are standardized, the industry can lower the cost of administrative overhead. A handful of transaction types make up the bulk of such interactions, including claims, remittance, eligibility inquiries, enrollment and disenrollment of plan members, as well as several others.

Congress directed the U.S. Department of Health and Human Services (HHS) to establish rules governing uniform record formats, code sets for diagnoses and procedures, and unique identifiers for healthcare providers, payers, and employers. This is an industry first, because Administrative Simplification covers all types of health plans and most providers, regardless of whether they are government-funded or private.

How HIPAA has evolved

To date, HHS has declared final rules governing transactions and code sets, employer identifiers, national provider identifiers, and enforcement. Each rule begins with a notice of proposed rule-making (NPRM) and a period for public response, after which a final rule is published in the *Federal Register*. Following publication of a given rule, organizations affected by Administrative Simplification have approximately two years (with some exceptions) to become compliant with that rule.

Congress recognized that, as the healthcare industry moves toward greater use of these standardized electronic transactions, new risks to patients' privacy and information security arise. Therefore, Congress further directed HHS to develop a Privacy Rule and a Security Rule, both of which are now enforceable.

Note that following the enforcement date of each final rule, HHS reserves the right to make annual modifications to a rule. As of this book's publication, the Privacy and Security rules have not been modified, but future changes are expected.

Important terms

All rules related to Administrative Simplification share several common terms that are important to understand. Please note that these definitions are simplified. For exact definitions, please refer to the Administrative Simplification section of the HIPAA legislation.

Covered entities

A covered entity (CE) is an individual who or organization that is subject to the rules of Administrative Simplification. CEs include all health plans, from traditional insurers, such as Blue Cross Blue Shield, to government programs, such as Medicare and Medicaid. CEs are also healthcare clearinghouses that often reformat and retransmit transactions for these entities. And finally, CEs are healthcare providers who engage in electronic transmission of any of these transactions. (Note that providers who are strictly paper-based or do not interact with insurance plans are not subject to the rules of Administrative Simplification.)

Protected health information (PHI)

Protected health information (PHI) is the information that CEs are required to protect and keep confidential through their privacy and security programs as specified in those rules. Essentially, it is any information that could reasonably be used to identify a given patient or plan member. PHI can appear in any form, including oral, paper, and electronic interactions.

Be aware that PHI goes beyond direct identifiers such as name, medical record number, and plan member ID, and may include indirect information which—when coupled with other information, such as publicly available census data—could be used to identify a person. In some cases, even a diagnosis code or an occupation can be enough information to reveal a person's identity. Note that PHI includes (and does not distinguish between) demographic, financial, and clinical data about a patient or plan member.

Designated record set

Designated record set (DRS) is a group of records maintained by or for a CE and used by the CE to make decisions about individuals. This broad record set includes providers' medical and billing records, as well as health plans' enrollment, payment, claims adjudication, and case management records. It also includes information received from other sources. In the case of a provider, this includes records received from another treatment provider. A DRS may be either in paper or electronic form.

Workforce

Workforce is a term used in the rules to include a CE's employees, as well as its unpaid volunteers, students, and even people who may be involved in the CE's training program. In short, workforce refers to any people working under the control of the CE, whether they're being paid or not. The rules clearly hold CEs responsible for training, compliance, and sanctions for their workforce. (Note that workforce members and business associates [see below] are mutually exclusive categories.)

Business associates

A business associate (BA) is a third party that assists a CE in performing its work involving PHI. For example, many providers use external transcription, coding, billing, and collections companies, all of which would qualify as BAs. And many CEs use accreditation agencies, legal firms, and software vendors that, in some cases, have access to PHI. Your marketing department may supply PHI to a telemarketing company, thus qualifying it as a BA. Because HHS does not have regulatory authority over these types of businesses, the rules hold CEs accountable, to some extent, for BAs' actions regarding protection of PHI. Note that in some instances, the BA is also a CE, in which case the BA is directly responsible for HIPAA compliance.

Common elements of HIPAA's Privacy and Security Rules

HIPAA's Privacy and Security Rules have many CE requirements in common. Both rules require

1. reasonable protections, in the form of written policies and procedures—the starting point for any formal privacy or security program

2. that a CE name a privacy official and an information security official as single points of responsibility for the programs

3. that the full workforce receive adequate training in the organization's privacy and security policies and procedures

4. CEs to anticipate privacy and security breaches, plan for mitigating harmful impacts of such breaches, and apply appropriate sanctions if the breach or violation is caused by a workforce member

5. that CEs identify their third-party BAs and have them sign privacy and security agreements (which may be combined into one document) as described in each rule

In addition, both of the privacy and security rules emphasize the requirement for formal (i.e., written) policies and procedures, incident reports, and other documentation. All such documents must be retained for at least six years from creation or last use (whichever is later) in case of civil action by the government.

Finally, the rules note that privacy and security programs are not one-time setup events, but are ongoing and dynamic. The rules allow for flexibility in how an organization complies, particularly in terms of security, but not whether it complies. CEs are expected to continue to monitor their compliance and update their practices as conditions change.

Your organization should already have policies and procedures that are compliant with these regulations. But, as you'll learn in this book, the stipulations on the subject of marketing may not be fully addressed by your organization's general HIPAA compliance efforts. Strategies for senior marketing professionals regarding training and monitoring compliance with HIPAA appear in Chapter 8.

Penalties and enforcement

There are both civil and criminal penalties associated with these rules.

Civil penalties

Civil penalties for noncompliance with any Administrative Simplification rules are monetary fines. They range from up to $100 per person per violation to a maximum of $25,000 per person for violation of a single standard in one calendar year. Note that there is no cap on the total amount of the civil penalties for violations of multiple regulations by a single organization.

Criminal penalties

Criminal penalties may be monetary or imprisonment, or both. Criminal penalties can be assessed for "wrongful disclosure" of PHI, "knowingly and in violation of HIPAA." Criminal acts involve using a person's identifier, obtaining PHI, or disclosing PHI contrary to HIPAA's regulations. The severity of the penalty increases if the act involves false pretenses, commercial advantage, personal gain, or malicious harm. The most serious acts can result in a fine of $250,000 and 10 years' imprisonment.

For more details about civil and criminal penalties associated with HIPAA violations, please refer to Appendix A.

Enforcement

At this time, enforcement is limited to investigation of complaints reported to HHS. Privacy complaints are handled by HHS's Office for Civil Rights. All other HIPAA complaints, including security complaints, are handled by HHS's Office of HIPAA Standards, which is within the Centers for Medicare & Medicaid Services (CMS). If either office believes there is criminal activity, they will turn the case over to the U.S. Department of Justice.

HHS has released an enforcement rule with details of the investigation process. It is worth noting that this rule states that any information obtained in a HIPAA investigation may be used by HHS for other purposes. The healthcare industry is already familiar with Medicare Fraud and Abuse investigations and penalties, for example, and should be alert to this condition.

The rule also states that it will make public any entity that is assessed a civil or criminal penalty.

Privacy principles and HIPAA's Privacy Rule

Privacy principles and HIPAA's Privacy Rule

As the field of consumer credit reporting evolved, unreasonable credit denials caused by inaccurate personal financial information grew, along with instances of misuse of personal information. With the advent of the Fair Credit Reporting Act (FCRA) in 1970, common principles underlying information privacy took shape in this country and in other nations.

The FCRA and other similar laws recognize the basic rights of consumers to know what personal information is being collected about them, how it is being used, and how errors can be corrected. At the same time, legislation imposed limits on organizations that collect consumers' personal data, obligating them to secure this data and keep it private.

Key privacy principles

The following principles provide the framework for an organization's consumer privacy protection efforts in this country and abroad. These principles are broad, universal goals applicable to anyone's personal information, whether financial, commercial, or medical. They are intended to protect citizens' privacy, and they appear in the laws of many nations and political entities, including the European Union.

- Transparency: Public documents describe the organization's policies governing what personal information it collects, how it is used or disclosed, and how it is protected.

- Collection: Information is collected with the knowledge (or at least the implicit consent) of the individual, and with an understanding of the purpose for the data collection.

- Disclosures: Uses and disclosures of personal information by the collecting organization must be related to the organization's main function(s). Otherwise, the individual must be given an opportunity to opt out or consent. There are exceptions, however, when it's

  - required or permitted by law
  - for investigation of the organization's compliance
  - for investigation of unlawful activities

Under some laws and regulations, the organization is required to document when certain of these exceptional uses and disclosures occur. Uses and disclosures should be governed by the "minimum necessary" principle; and, when feasible, de-identified data should be used instead of individually identifiable data.

- Subject access: The organization must grant access to personal information in response to reasonable requests from individuals who are the subject of the information. If access is denied for certain limited reasons, the organization must give the reason. Charges for access, if any, must not be excessive. If the individual disputes the validity or completeness of his or her information, there must be a straightforward process for correction.

- Data quality: The organization must take steps to reasonably assure that personal information is accurate, complete, and up to date (as relevant to the organization's purposes).

- Data security: The organization must take steps to reasonably assure the confidentiality, integrity, and availability of the personal information it maintains. The organization must collect only what is needed, and must destroy data when it is no longer needed for its legitimate purposes.

The HIPAA Privacy Rule writers were quite familiar with these principles and incorporated them into the rule. These requirements fall into the category of either (a) patients' and plan members' rights or (b) organizations' obligations.

Patients' and plan members' rights

The privacy rights described in general terms above are expressed in specific terms in HIPAA's Privacy Rule. The Rule has given patients and health plan members across the country new universal rights. Those rights are detailed below.

The right to receive a privacy notice explaining how the CE uses and disclos-es protected health information (PHI), what rights individuals have, and how to exercise those rights [§164.520]

The Privacy Rule gives detailed instructions regarding the content of a covered entity's (CE) privacy notice (or "notice of privacy practices"). Every privacy notice must carry the header, "THIS NOTICE DESCRIBES HOW MEDICAL INFORMATION ABOUT YOU MAY BE USED AND DISCLOSED AND HOW YOU CAN GET ACCESS TO THIS INFORMATION. PLEASE REVIEW IT CAREFULLY." It must describe generally whom your organization includes (that is, who will have access to PHI), and it must include examples of certain uses that are permitted without any special agreement by the individual.

It must also list other potential uses and disclosures by the organization that are permitted by HIPAA and do not require authorization—for example, a healthcare provider that is required to report certain conditions to state health agencies.

It must state that all other uses and disclosures of PHI are permitted only with the individual's explicit authorization.

The privacy notice must spell out patient (and plan member) rights under HIPAA's Privacy Rule, and it must identify a contact person for inquiries related to the notice and privacy rights and complaints.

Beyond the privacy notice content, the rule specifies how the notice must be communicated to patients and plan members. Note that the privacy notice is a public document and must be provided to anyone who asks for a copy.

Patients

The full notice must be posted prominently (e.g., on a waiting room wall, on a company Web site). Each new patient must be handed a privacy notice and must be asked to sign or initial an acknowledgment of receipt of the notice. All returning patients also are required to receive the notice and sign an acknowledgement at the time of the first date of service following the rule enforcement date in April 2003. There is no requirement to mail privacy notices to old (pre-existing) patients who have not returned since April 2003. However, if an old patient calls in for a consultation or prescription refill, for example, and has not received the notice, it must be mailed to the patient with a request to sign and return the acknowledgment form.

As long as the privacy notice contains a statement that the CE reserves the right to change the terms of its notice and make the new terms effective for all PHI, the revised notice does not need to be handed out to each patient post-revisions. However, it must replace the old notice wherever it is posted.

Plan members

Unlike the patient-provider relationship, it is assumed that plan members have little direct physical contact with their health plan. Hence, there is no requirement to hand out privacy notices. Instead, health plans are required to post the notice on their Web site and mail a paper version to its members as of the rule enforcement date, to new members upon enrollment, and within 60 days of a material revision to covered members. At least once every three years, each plan is required to notify its members of the notice and how to obtain a copy.

The right to access information the CE has about the individual, at no charge [§ 164.524]

Information in the broadly defined designated record set (DRS) held by a CE must be open to inspection by the subject of the data, with a limited number of exceptions. The method of access is left up to each organization and may be electronic or printed. CEs must not limit this access to the traditional medical record, for example, since the DRS encompasses more, including billing records and sometimes digital images. Access (or denial, with reason for denial) must be granted within 30 days of the request. CEs may not assess a fee for this important right.

The right to receive a copy of that information at a reasonable, cost-based charge [§ 164.524]

Patients and plan members may choose to receive a copy of part or all of their DRS. CEs may ask if the patient or plan member prefers a copy of a subset of the DRS, such as information related to a hospital stay or other encounter. CEs may also offer a summary of the information if the patient agrees and agrees to any fee.

While CEs may charge for this service, fees must be reasonable and cost-based. That is, fees may only include the cost of copying, postage (if the individual requests that the information be mailed), and preparing a summary if the individual has agreed to it. Otherwise, the fee may become a barrier to the individual exercising his or her right.

It is important for every CE to thoroughly understand and follow the regulations regarding time frames for responding, permissible reasons for denial, and the denial review process.

The right to request amendment of that information if it is believed to be incorrect or incomplete [§ 164.526]

Occasionally, when individuals review their information, they believe there is an omission or error. The CE must support a process for receiving and reviewing requests for amendment of PHI. The CE is not required to apply the amendment, but there are rules governing fair review and denial of such requests. If the CE agrees to amend PHI, it must reasonably ensure that all copies of the relevant PHI are amended. This is important for data integrity and can affect patient care.

The right to request restrictions on the use or disclosure of that information [§ 164.522]

Individuals may request that their PHI not be used or disclosed for various purposes, including treatment, payment, and healthcare operations. But CEs are not required to agree. Even if a CE agrees, there are exceptions, such as in a medical emergency. Hence, this is a rather weak right, but it attempts to give individuals a measure of control over their personal information. And there may be specific instances when it is warranted.

The right to a report of certain disclosures of that information [§ 164.528]

If individuals are concerned about an inappropriate disclosure of their personal health information, they may request an accounting of disclosures. CEs must maintain a record of certain disclosures for a period of six years in case this information is requested. Individuals are entitled to one report per year without charge.

CEs are not required to include in the report disclosures for the purposes of treatment, payment, and healthcare operations. Individuals are given notice of these types of disclosures in each CE's privacy notice. Also, disclosures that the individual has agreed to by signing an authorization form are not required in the report.

The report must show for each disclosure:

- The date of the disclosure

- The name of the entity or person who received the PHI

- A brief description of the PHI disclosed

- A brief statement of the purpose for the disclosure

The right to request confidential communications from the organization [§ 164.522]

Patients and plan members may request that communications be made to an alternate address or telephone number, for example, for greater privacy.

Providers must accommodate all such reasonable requests and may not require an explanation. Plans must also accommodate such requests if individuals state that disclosure of their PHI could endanger them.

The right to refuse to authorize certain uses and disclosures of PHI, and the right to revoke an earlier authorization [§ 164.508]

When a CE wishes to use or disclose PHI for reasons other than treatment, payment, or healthcare operations, or for public health and other (usually required by regulation) similar public-good reasons, the CE must first obtain a voluntary written authorization from the individual. This requirement is clearly explained in each CE's privacy notice so that patients and plan members understand how their information will be used and disclosed. Any other purpose for a use or disclosure of PHI must be clearly stated in an authorization form.

The Privacy Rule contains specific requirements for a valid authorization form, and each CE is obligated to comply. The form must carry a statement indicating that signing is voluntary and that the authorization may be revoked if the individual later changes his or her mind (although action taken while the authorization was in effect cannot be undone). This right gives the individual complete control over uses and disclosures not directly related to CEs' core functions of providing and paying for healthcare.

The right to opt out of a facility directory [§ 164.510]

Patients who are residents in an inpatient facility, such as a hospital, are generally listed in a facility directory containing basic information such as the person's condition and room location. When a visitor calls or appears, the facility may share this information with a visitor who asks for the patient by name. Patients also may provide a religious preference, which can lead to a clergy visit. Upon admission this practice must be explained to patients so that they can choose to opt out of the directory if they so wish. Some patients may prefer to keep that information private—even from family members. Facilities generally can make arrangements for communications with visitors the patient wishes to see, even if the patient has opted out of the directory.

The right to opt out of fundraising communications [§ 164.514]

Providers may use limited patient information to send fundraising communications, but the letter must clearly state that patients have the right to opt out of any further such communications. And CEs must honor that request.

The right to file a complaint without retaliation—with either the CE or the Secretary of HHS [§ 160.306, §164.520]

A person who believes a CE is not complying with the Privacy Rule may file a complaint with the Secretary of HHS or with the CE. This right must be included in each CE's privacy notice, along with a statement explaining that there will be no retaliation for taking this action. This is a particularly important right, because, at this time, rule enforcement is strictly through complaints filed by individuals. The government does not perform routine audits of CEs to determine their compliance levels.

Covered entities' organizational obligations

There are other obligations CEs must take on to comply with the Privacy Rule. A CE's information privacy program must entail a formal structure starting with a privacy official to oversee key elements of the program, including policy development and implementation, workforce training, and compliance monitoring.

CEs must provide extensive administrative processes and documents in support of all the privacy rights described above. Written policies and procedures form the basis of the administrative processes, from which workforce and technology processes evolve. These policies codify privacy principles such as the responsibility to access only that information needed to do one's job: the "minimum necessary" and "need to know" principles. CEs also should use de-identified data instead of personally identifiable data when possible for a given task.

The workforce needs to understand the policies, how they are expected to act, and the consequences or sanctions for violations. These items should be conveyed in workforce training programs that are periodic, rather than a one-time event. (See Chapter 8.) Because the details of the Privacy Rule are sometimes complicated, the workforce should understand that, if unsure, it is best to question a potential use or disclosure and refer it to the privacy official.

CEs are also obligated to identify their business associates (BAs), as defined by HIPAA, and ensure that all BAs sign a HIPAA-compliant BA agreement concerning both privacy and security of the PHI they may collect or access on behalf of the CE. Although the rule stops short of requiring CEs to audit their BAs, it is good practice to discuss privacy and security with BAs and review their policies and processes. CEs must be prepared to respond to privacy and security violations and breaches occurring within a BA's domain, because the CE may suffer the consequences—both in terms of government penalties and public reaction.

The Privacy Rule contains what is sometimes referred to as a mini–security rule, which recognizes that privacy requires security and requires administrative, physical, and technical safeguards (i.e., security measures) to protect all forms of PHI.

Finally, HIPAA has an indirect impact on some employers that are not CEs, through their sponsorship of group health plans for employees.

It is important for each organization to investigate and learn whether or not the privacy and security rules affect them through their human resources or benefits department's use of employee data from the plan, such as employee health claims, or from medical reimbursement accounts.

Other preemptive state and federal privacy laws

HIPAA's Privacy Rule describes when and under what conditions CEs may use and disclose PHI, and explains patients' and plan members' privacy rights. It is important to point out, however, that there are other laws and regulations at the federal and state levels that also address information privacy.

The HIPAA Privacy Rule writers carefully avoid conflicts with other federal laws, such as the Federal Educational Rights and Privacy Act (FERPA), and explain the intersection in detail in the rule's preamble.

As to state laws and regulations, the general rule is that the HIPAA Privacy Rule preempts or takes precedence over weaker laws, thus creating a uniform national baseline for health information privacy protections. Where there are stronger state laws and regulations that are consistent with HIPAA, such laws prevail in those states. When such a law conflicts with HIPAA, the secretary of HHS makes a decision. Thus, CEs that operate in multiple states must continue to follow separate laws and regulations in some cases.

HIPAA's Security Rule

HIPAA's Security Rule

HIPAA's Security Rule applies only to protected health information (PHI) in electronic form (a.k.a. ePHI). This is due to the Administrative Simplification section's focus on standardization of the electronic transactions that flow through the industry, such as claims and insured's eligibility (or insurance coverage for specific healthcare services). However, because of the mini–security rule within the Privacy Rule, covered entities' (CEs') security programs should encompass all forms of PHI (and, in this interconnected world, other protected information assets).

The Security Rule begins with general requirements, which are followed by separate sections covering administrative, physical, and technical safeguards.

General requirements

The Security Rule contains several general requirements for CEs.

1. Ensure the confidentiality, integrity, and availability of ePHI

2. Protect against any reasonably anticipated threats or hazards to the security of ePHI

3. Protect against any reasonably anticipated uses and disclosures that are not permitted or required by the Privacy Rule

4. Ensure workforce compliance

Information security is often defined as the assurance of confidentiality, integrity, and availability of protected information assets. The Security Rule writers remind the healthcare industry of this definition in its general requirements. Confidentiality means restricting access to certain information, so that only people and processes authorized to access the data are able to. Data integrity is the assurance that data has not been inappropriately altered or destroyed, either by a person or a computer process. Availability ensures that the information is accessible when it is needed by those authorized to access it. Each of the rule's standards works to support one or more of these three goals.

The rule specifically allows for flexibility in how a CE complies with the rule's standards or requirements. This is only reasonable, since CEs range from small offices to very large, multi-state organizations. CEs may use any measures to reasonably and appropriately implement the rule's standards, taking into account the organization's size, complexity, capabilities, and cost. In this case, "cost" refers to the cost of the security measure as compared to the level of risk and cost of mitigating any harmful impact of a security breach. Security measures should always be linked to the probability and criticality of the risks they are intended to mitigate. Realistically, implementing security measures is not cost-free.

The rule's requirements are technology-neutral. This allows organizations to make their own technology decisions. And it accommodates new technologies as they arise, without requiring rule updates. The downside to this approach is that the language of the rule is sometimes abstract, leaving room for unintentional loopholes.

The Security Rule emphasizes that CEs' compliance efforts must be ongoing, and not be a one-time event. Indeed, security can only be maintained when security processes are monitored and periodically reviewed and revised.

Administrative safeguards

The administrative requirements are placed before the physical and technical ones because the former are the basis for the latter, and because without administrative processes, the physical and technical safeguards have limited effect. There are also many more administrative requirements than physical or technical ones.

Note that some administrative requirements are quite similar to Privacy Rule requirements and are discussed separately in Chapter 1.

The first administrative section standard says it all: Security Management Process. This includes risk assessment and risk management, a sanction policy for violations, and regular review of activity within computer systems containing ePHI. Managing risk—that is, identifying risks, protecting against them, identifying and responding to security incidents, mitigating any harmful impact, and retrospectively examining controls to look for improvement—is what constitutes every reasonable security program.

CEs are required to know and control their workforce through a clearance process, making sure they are appropriately authorized for access to PHI, and ensuring there is an effective and timely termination process for suspending physical and computer access to PHI when it is no longer authorized. CEs must have a well-documented process for granting computer system access and setting up user IDs and privileges.

Workforce training must be formalized and documented and must include topics such as the CE's key security policies and principles, how to avoid malicious software, and how to manage passwords or other forms of user authentication. The workforce must know how to recognize and report suspected security incidents, as well as how to follow safe behavior, such as logging off computers and locking up confidential materials before leaving the work area. The workforce must also be informed about the sanctions their organization can impose, and the potential for external sanctions, such as legal action and reporting to HHS. To reinforce security principles, CEs must issue periodic reminders to its workforce.

Businesses and agencies today recognize the need for a contingency plan in case of a disaster that affects computer systems. CEs are required to develop and maintain such a plan, which must include a criticality analysis to identify the most essential or time-sensitive systems, back-up procedures, and disaster recovery plans that are periodically tested.

Because compliance is largely self-regulated, CEs are required to periodically audit their compliance with the Security Rule. This can be done by either internal staff or a third party. Deficiencies should be identified and addressed.

Physical safeguards

According to the National Institute of Standards and Technology (NIST), risks to computer systems come from three sources of risk: natural (such as hurricanes), environmental (such as burst water mains), and human (insiders and outsiders, with and without malicious intent). All three risk sources can be partially controlled through the use of physical controls.

CEs are required to implement facility access controls, such as a facility security plan that might include locks and cameras, verifying the identity of staff and visitors entering the facility and limiting their access to restricted areas such as the computer center, and reviewing construction plans to ensure that no physical vulnerability is inadvertently created.

HIPAA makes the CE responsible for its ePHI wherever it is and wherever its workers are. Hence, CEs must implement policies and procedures for protecting their workstations that can be used to access PHI. This includes all end-user devices, from desktops and laptops to PDAs and thumb drives, at work, at home, and on the road. CEs must also implement procedures for protecting workstations' surroundings, where confidential documents and media may be exposed. With the slew of news reports of lost and stolen laptops and other devices, organizations are increasingly requiring encryption and physical lock-up of portable devices and media, although these precautions are not explicitly required in the rule.

Also in the news are reports of discovery of confidential data that should have been destroyed. The rule requires CEs to implement sound disposal practices to ensure that ePHI is adequately destroyed, for example, prior to donating old computers or throwing out unwanted disks. And although this rule focuses on electronic data, the Privacy Rule makes clear that CEs must also safely destroy paper documents containing PHI, as well.

Technical safeguards

The rule's technical safeguards encompass access controls, electronic audit controls, data integrity mechanisms, and transmission security. It should be noted that many additional technical measures are standard practice today, such as network perimeter firewalls. The fact that they are not explicitly mentioned in the rule should not be construed as condoning the lack of reasonable and acceptable security controls in an organization.

Access controls are central to security. Each computer user accessing a protected resource containing ePHI must have his or her own unique user ID and an acceptable form of user authentication, most often a password.

CEs must keep and monitor audit trails to identify any suspicious activity in systems containing ePHI.

The integrity of ePHI is critical in healthcare. If, for example, a patient's lab results are changed—either by accident or maliciously—harm could come to the patient. Some integrity mechanisms are built into database systems, software, and network protocols. CEs must identify and assess the adequacy of these and other available integrity mechanisms.

Finally, encryption is cited as a technical safeguard in the rule. However, CEs have some latitude in determining when encryption is used. It is generally accepted that encryption is the only way to ensure confidentiality when transmitting ePHI over the Internet and over wireless networks today.

How HIPAA defines and treats marketing

4

How HIPAA defines and treats marketing

The goal of marketing is to communicate a consistent, intended message to a specific target audience in order to cause an action, such as a purchase, or to increase the public's knowledge concerning a topic. There are two general approaches:

1. Place the message where the desired audience is likely to see it, such as through print, broadcast, Internet, and other mass media outlets

2. Identify specific members of the target audience and deliver the message directly to them, commonly called database marketing

Marketing intersects with HIPAA in the second approach, when specific people—identified patients and plan members—are the targeted recipients of a marketing communication.

Studies indicate that it is much easier and cheaper to sell to existing customers than it is to win over new ones. Covered entities (CEs) already have a relationship with their patients or plan members, and those people are more likely to pay attention to information from a familiar source. That fact makes it very tempting for CEs to use the personal data at hand for their marketing purposes.

While this chapter will delve into the Privacy Rule's definition of marketing, special carve-outs, and exceptions, it is important to keep in mind that HIPAA's view of marketing does not consistently match what CEs consider marketing. That is, some common marketing projects are not considered marketing by HIPAA, while other efforts within a CE, be it in the community relations office or business development department, for instance, may qualify as marketing under HIPAA's definition.

To further complicate matters, sometimes HIPAA requires authorization for what it defines as marketing and sometimes it does not. Also, HIPAA may or may not require authorization for activities that it does not consider marketing but that are thought of as marketing by CEs, depending on whether and how protected health information (PHI) is used or disclosed. Hence, it is strongly recommended that all database marketing initiatives undertaken by a CE be carefully reviewed with the CE's privacy official in advance. There are recommendations in Chapter 8 for senior marketing professionals who are uneasy or unsure about how to work with their organization's privacy official.

HIPAA's definition of marketing

HIPAA's Privacy Rule defines marketing as the following:

"To make a communication about a product or service that encourages recipients of the communication to purchase or use the product or service."

In general, the Privacy Rule requires prior authorization (as defined by the rule) from the patient or plan member before his or her PHI is to be used to identify targets for marketing initiatives.

Not marketing!

The rule identifies many common communications between CEs and their patients and plan members that are not defined as marketing. Instead, these communications are considered treatment or healthcare operations, even if they benefit the CE financially.

This seems to contradict the conventional definition of marketing, so it is important to note what the rule says and to review its examples in order to understand some fine distinctions.

Three types of communications are cited as nonmarketing and therefore acceptable without any particular agreement by the recipient. These include when a CE communicates to individuals about

1. the participating providers and health plans in a network, the services offered by a provider, or the benefits covered by a health plan

2. the individual's treatment

3. case management or care coordination for that individual, or directions or recommendations for alternative treatments, therapies, health care providers, or setting of care for that individual

As long as the CE's use of PHI fits one of the above scenarios, the CE is free to make the communication without first obtaining an authorization from the patient or plan member who will receive the communication.

HHS intentionally does not include all instances of treatment, payment, and healthcare operations in the above exclusions from the marketing definition. The specific communications listed above were carved out to "enhance the individual's access to quality health care." The rule writers noted that the public strongly objects to commercial use of their PHI to try to sell products and services, even if they are health-related, beyond the fundamental communications listed above. Hence, other communications between CEs and individuals, even if they fall under the definition of payment and operations, may be considered marketing.

The following are examples of these permissible uses and disclosures, according to HHS.

Communications from a provider

Examples of permissible communications include

- a provider who refers an individual to a specialist

- a doctor who writes a prescription for a patient

- a provider who mails a prescription refill reminder to a patient (even if the provider is compensated by a third party)

- appointment reminders sent to patients

- communications to patients about disease management

- information about new diagnostic tools

Scenario: The wellness program

Q A hospital engages a business associate (BA) to establish and manage a wellness program. The wellness program features a weight-loss clinic. The hospital sends a letter to all its obese patients seen over the past year, informing them about the new clinic. As the hospital selected patients using clinical criteria (weight), is this acceptable under HIPAA?

A Yes. A CE may use its PHI as necessary to identify appropriate subpopulations for its nonmarketing communications—as long as they're for health-related products or services, wellness programs, disease management, etc. And the fact that the wellness program is managed by another organization is not a problem, because it is essentially an extension of the hospital and covered by a BA agreement.

Communications from a health plan

The rule allows health plans to communicate with plan members about health insurance products offered by the plan when they could enhance or replace the recipient's existing health plan coverage. For example, if a child is about to "age out" of coverage under a family health insurance policy, the plan may send information about continuation coverage for the child.

Note that the communications must be about health-related products or services, and they must be about such products or services available only to a health plan enrollee when those products or services add value to a benefit plan.

Health plan value-added items and services (VAIS) must meet two criteria to qualify as nonmarketing communications...

1. The value-added items must be health-related.

For example, offering a discount for eyeglasses is acceptable, but not movie theater tickets.

2. The value-added items must "demonstrably add value to the plan's membership and not merely be a pass-through of a discount or item available to the public at large."

For example, offering a discount for a health club membership is acceptable, but not if plan members could obtain the same discount directly from the club.

It is important to recognize that the above exclusions from HIPAA's definition of marketing, such as communications about a CE's health-related products and services, may fall squarely in a CE's marketing department. This simply means that these specific activities are permitted under HIPAA without taking any special measures.

Marketing!

The following are examples of marketing, as defined by HIPAA. Each of the following requires prior explicit authorization from every targeted patient or plan member.

Communications from a provider that require authorization

- A mailing to patients encouraging them to discuss an alternative product when it is paid for by a pharmaceutical company with the intent of marketing that product

- A home health nurse or physical therapist acting as a marketer for durable medical equipment companies

Communications from a health plan requiring authorization

- A mailing to members about other, nonhealth lines of insurance, such as life or disability insurance (This is considered marketing because it is not health-related.)

- Mailing discount coupons to a local movie theater (This is considered marketing because it is not health-related.)

- Mailing discount coupons a local health club when plan members can get the discount directly from the club (This is marketing because the VAIS is available independent of plan membership.)

Remuneration doesn't define marketing

Some permissible communications, such as mailing prescription refill reminders, may result in financial benefits to the CE. HHS states that the receipt of remuneration alone should not "transform a treatment communication into a commercial promotion of a product or service. For example, health care providers should be able to, and can, send patients prescription refill reminders regardless of whether a third party pays or subsidizes the communication." HHS further states that a CE may engage a BA to assist it in making permissible communications. "It is only in situations where, in the guise of a BA, an entity other than the CE is promoting its own products using PHI it has received from, and for which it has paid, the CE, that the remuneration will place the activity within HIPAA's definition of marketing."

BAs, other third parties, and marketing

A CE may engage mail houses, telemarketers, and other businesses to perform marketing activities on its behalf. If the CE does not release or give the business access to its PHI, then this business relationship is outside the scope of HIPAA.

On the other hand, if the CE discloses PHI to the business in this context, then the business becomes a HIPAA-defined BA. Under this special designation, the BA must sign a special BA contract before the CE may release any PHI. For a list of essential and recommended components of a BA contract, see Appendix B.

In addition to other specific privacy and security terms of this contract, the BA must agree to use and disclose the CE's PHI only when acting on behalf of the CE for *agreed-upon services*. In other words, the BA may not use the

PHI for its own marketing or other purposes (unless the CE has first obtained an explicit authorization from each individual).

HHS bars the potential for manipulating the BA relationship to circumvent privacy protections by defining marketing expressly to include "an arrangement between a covered entity and any other entity whereby the covered entity discloses protected health information to the other entity ... for the other entity or its affiliate to make a communication about its own product or service that encourages recipients of the communication to purchase or use that product or service." These communications are marketing and can occur only if the CE obtains the individual's authorization. HHS believes its definition of marketing clearly expresses the "fundamental prohibition against covered entities selling lists of patients or enrollees to third parties, or from disclosing protected health information to a third party for the marketing activities of the third party, without the written authorization of the individual."

Marketing compliance is about more than just HIPAA

According to the U.S. Department of Health and Human Services, "nothing in the marketing provisions of the Privacy Rule is to be construed as amending, modifying, or changing any rule or requirement related to any other federal or state statutes or regulations, including specifically anti-kickback, fraud and abuse, or self-referral statutes or regulations, or to authorize or permit any activity or transaction currently proscribed by such statutes and regulations."

This means that, even if the Privacy Rule's marketing section permits certain patient and plan member communications without requiring authorization, CEs must still follow all other applicable federal and state laws. For example, in any marketing communications that recommend alternative treatments or alternative-treatment facilities to a patient, the provider must keep in mind fraud and anti-kickback laws and regulations. For a more detailed discussion of pre emptive federal and state laws, refer to Chapter 2.

The HHS continues, "Examples of such laws include the anti-kickback statute (section 1128B(b) of the Social Security Act), safe harbor regulations (42 CFR part 1001), Stark law (section 1877 of the Social Security Act) and regulations (42 CFR parts 411 and 424), and HIPAA statute on self-referral (section 1128C of the Social Security Act).

"The definition of marketing is solely applicable to the Privacy Rule and the permissions granted by the Rule are only for a covered entity's use or disclosure of protected health information. In particular, although this regulation defines the term 'marketing' to exclude communications to an individual to recommend, purchase, or use a product or service as part of the treatment of the individual or for case management or care coordination of that individual, such communication by a 'white coat' health care professional may violate the anti-kickback statute. Similar examples for pharmacist communications with patients relating to the marketing of products on behalf of pharmaceutical companies were identified by the OIG as problematic in a 1994 Special Fraud Alert (December 19, 1994, 59 FR 65372).

"Other violations have involved home health nurses and physical therapists acting as marketers for durable medical equipment companies. **Although a particular communication under the Privacy Rule may not require patient authorization because it is not marketing, or may require patient authorization because it is 'marketing' as the Rule defines it, the arrangement may nevertheless violate other statutes and regulations administered by HHS, the Department of Justice, or other federal or state agency."**

The HHS further notes that "manufacturers that receive identifiable health information and misuse it may be subject to action taken under other consumer protection statutes by other federal agencies, such as the Federal Trade Commission."

Exceptions to the authorization requirement

The Privacy Rule generally requires authorization prior to use or disclosure of PHI for marketing. However, the rule recognizes two special situations that are defined as marketing but do not require authorization:

1. When the communication occurs in a face-to-face encounter between the CE and the individual

2. When the communication involves a promotional gift of nominal value

1. Face-to-face marketing

Note that this exception applies only to face-to-face encounters, not to letters, e-mail, phone, or fax messages. The rule writers made this exception so as not to interfere with the doctor- (or other provider-) patient relationship by forcing the provider to first obtain an authorization. A prime example is when a doctor gives a free product sample to a patient to try. HHS believes that individuals can stop or ignore unwanted face-to-face marketing communications.

The face-to-face marketing exception only applies to communications from a CE or from a CE's BA when that BA is acting on behalf of the CE. For example, an insurance agent who is a BA of a health plan may have a face-to-face encounter with a plan member when going "door to door" and marketing nonhealth insurance policies to plan members.

As demonstrated in the preceding example, the face-to-face encounter may involve marketing of nonhealth-related products or services, in which case it still does not require authorization.

2. Promotional gifts of nominal value

In this exception to the authorization requirement, HHS suggests that, because the gifts are of nominal value, they should not unduly influence recipients.

Qualifying promotional gifts include items such as pens, note pads, cups, or calendars displaying the name of a product or company. As with the face-to-face marketing exception, it is assumed that the gift is distributed by the CE or the CE's BA acting on behalf of the CE. In this way, no PHI is released to a third party for any other use.

Scenario: Dental hygiene gifts

Q The local dentist's office hands out a toothbrush, a small tube of toothpaste, and a travel size package of dental floss whenever a patient comes in for a dental cleaning. Because these products carry particular brand names, is this considered marketing? If so, is it permitted without first obtaining an authorization?

A Yes, this is considered marketing under HIPAA, but it is permitted without authorization because it involves a promotional gift of nominal value from the provider, a CE.

Authorization
requirements

Authorization requirements

HIPAA's Privacy Rule states that as a general rule, "except as otherwise permitted or required by this subchapter, a covered entity may not use or disclose protected health information without an authorization that is valid under this section. When a covered entity obtains or receives a valid authorization for its use or disclosure of protected health information, such use or disclosure must be consistent with such authorization."

When a covered entity (CE) requests authorization to use or disclose protected health information (PHI) for the purpose of marketing (by the CE or a third party) to its patients or plan members, an authorization must contain the following elements to be deemed valid:

- A description of the purpose of the requested use or disclosure of PHI

- If the marketing involves direct or indirect remuneration to the CE from a third party, a statement that the requested use or disclosure involves direct or indirect remuneration to the CE

- A description of the information to be used or disclosed, identifying the information in a specific and meaningful fashion

- Name or other specific identification of the person(s) or class of person(s) authorized to make the requested use or disclosure

- Name or other specific identification of the person(s) or class of person(s) to whom the CE may make the requested use or disclosure

- An expiration date or expiration event that relates to the individual or the purpose of the requested use or disclosure

- A statement that the individual may inspect or copy the PHI to be used or disclosed

- A statement that the individual may refuse to sign the authorization

- A statement that treatment, payment, enrollment, or eligibility for benefits may not be conditioned on obtaining the authorization (i.e., treatment, payment, etc., will not be affected if the individual refuses to sign)

- A statement of the individual's right to revoke the authorization in writing, except when the CE has already acted on it, and a description of how the individual may revoke the authorization (or reference to the CE's privacy notice if it contains instructions)

- A statement that information used or disclosed pursuant to the authorization may be subject to redisclosure by the recipient, and may no longer be protected by the Privacy Rule

- Signature of the individual and date

- If the authorization is signed by a personal representative of the individual, a description of the representative's authority to act for the individual

Additional requirements for a valid marketing authorization are

- the authorization must be written in plain language

- the required statements must be written so that the individual can understand their substance

- The authorization may not be combined with another, different form

An authorization is not valid if it has any of the following defects:

- The expiration date has passed or the expiration event is known by the CE to have occurred

- The authorization has not been filled out completely

- The authorization is known by the CE to have been revoked

- The authorization lacks one or more of the required elements

- Any material information in the authorization is known by the CE to be false

Finally, HHS makes clear that a blanket marketing authorization is not permitted. The requirements listed above are intended to "give individuals sufficient information and notice regarding the type of use or disclosure of their protected health information that they are authorizing. Without such specificity, an authorization would not have meaning. Indeed, blanket marketing authorizations would be considered defective...."

When an authorization is completed and signed, the CE must give a copy to the individual.

Note: Please note that the list of required elements above and the sample form below apply to use or disclosure of PHI for marketing. The Privacy Rule requirements for an authorization vary for some other use/disclosure purposes.

Figure 5.1 is an example of an authorization form for marketing. It has been completed by the CE, the fictional Central City General Hospital, but the patient has not yet initialed and signed the form. (This form was adapted from a model form provided by HHS.)

Figure 5.1   AUTHORIZATION FORM

AUTHORIZATION FOR RELEASE OF INFORMATION
Central City General Hospital
300 1st Avenue, Central City, PA 15229

Section A: Must be completed for all authorizations
I hereby authorize the use or disclosure of my individually identifiable health information as described below. I understand that this authorization is voluntary. I understand that if the organization authorized to receive the information is not a health plan or health care provider, the released information may no longer be protected by federal privacy regulations.

Patient name: ___Janet Doe_____ ID Number: _____321-45-99_____

Persons/organizations providing the information: Persons/organizations receiving the information:
____Central City General Hospital _____   ____BrandX Pharmaceuticals_____
____Health Information Management Dept._____   ____Marketing Dept._____
_____   ____100 Main St., Big City, NJ 08723_____
_____   _____

Specific description of information (including date(s) if applicable):
Your name, mailing address, sex, and date of birth
_____
_____

Section B: Must be completed only if Central City General Hospital has requested the authorization

1. Central City General Hospital must complete the following:
    a. What is the purpose of the use or disclosure?: ___to provide marketing subjects to the BrandX Pharm. company
      for their new products_____

2. The patient or the patient's representative must read and initial the following statements:
    a. I understand that my health care and the payment for my health care will not be affected if fl do not sign this form.
                             Initials: _____
    b. I understand that I may see and copy the information described on this form if I ask for it, and that I
      get a copy of this form after I sign it.
                             Initials: _____
    c. I understand that Central City General Hospital is involved in direct or indirect financial compensation
      in exchange for using or disclosing my health information described above.   Initials: _____

Section C: Must be completed for all authorizations

The patient or the patient's representative must read and initial the following statements:
1. I understand that this authorization will expire on ___/___/_____(DD/MM/YEAR) or after the following event:
   _Data sent to recipient (which will occur on or before Oct. 1, 2006)_____   Initials: _____
2. I understand that I may revoke this authorization at any time by notifying Central City General Hospital in writing.
   But if I do, it won't have any effect on any actions they took before they received the revocation.
                             Initials: _____

_____   _____
Signature of patient or patient's representative   Date
(Form MUST be completed before initialing and signing.)
Printed name of patient's representative: _____
Relationship to the patient: _____
                * YOU MAY REFUSE TO SIGN THIS AUTHORIZATION *

Using patient data under HIPAA

Using patient data under HIPAA

Practically speaking, covered entities (CEs) have numerous opportunities to use protected health information (PHI) in their own marketing and public relations initiatives without running afoul of HIPAA.

Using PHI in ways that do not require authorization

It is likely to be more efficient and cost-effective for CEs to use PHI in ways that do not require authorization than in ways that do require it. But it is important for CEs to understand the restrictions associated with that decision and stay within the limits of such uses and disclosures of PHI.

Provider-to-patient communications about the patient's treatment and care coordination are likely to be unique situations, and, therefore, may not be the most useful marketing vector. But permissible provider and health plan communications about their health-related services and benefits are typically broad mailings to all or to groups of their patients and plan members. These communications can also indirectly promote the organization.

Examples include

- notice of the opening of a new women's health center, sports medicine practice, or other specialty program

- general annual or quarterly "newsletter" that discusses major points/pushes (e.g., new physicians, new specialty center, reminders about flex money, etc.)

- reminders to women to get an annual mammogram

- information about how to lower cholesterol

- notice of health fairs

- notice of wellness classes and support groups

- health plan updated book of network physicians

- notice of discount on health club membership, exclusive to plan members

In addition, CEs may distribute promotional gifts of nominal value, such as a calendar with the CE's name and photographs, to patients and plan members without authorization.

Other examples of uses of PHI to achieve marketing goals may or may not be considered marketing, but they still may not require CEs to obtain authorizations. For example, one latent marketing tactic is including statement stuffers or information sheets with patient bills and other patient mailings. Also, most medical billing systems include space in which to place a "marketing message" or reminder on the bill itself. This is a cost-effective way to reach current patients who are already receiving the CE's mailings. Just be sure that the message content in any patient or plan member mailing is consistent with the Privacy Rule's permitted uses of PHI as described in this book.

Scenario: The upsell

Q An ophthalmologist determines a patient needs cataract surgery. As the patient schedules the surgery, the doctor attempts to persuade the patient to choose a lens upgrade from what is normally covered by insurance. The doctor says it's a better product for this patient's particular medical condition and the patient will have a better outcome. Is this a violation of HIPAA's Privacy Rule regarding marketing and use of PHI?

A No. On the face of it, this appears to be a treatment communication. Even if the doctor has a financial incentive in promoting the more expensive lens, a face-to-face marketing communication between provider and patient is permitted by HIPAA without authorization. (Be aware of violating other laws, however!)

Scenario: The gift

Q A hospital sets up an arrangement with a local gym so that the gym will provide a free one-month trial membership to any of the hospital's cardiac patients who present a "One Month Free!" coupon. The gym doesn't offer this special program to anyone else. The hospital mails the coupons to its cardiac patients, explaining the offer and the health benefits of regular exercise in a supervised environment. Is this a violation of HIPAA?

A No. Because the hospital is offering a health-related benefit to its patients, and one that is not available to the general public, it appears to be permissible by HIPAA without authorization.

Scenario: The satisfaction survey

Q A hospital creates a list from its database of all mothers who have given birth in the past 12 months, and mails a survey asking about their maternity experience. Is this permissible under HIPAA without authorization?

A Yes. Whether the CE defines this as marketing or as healthcare operations (if this survey is part of a performance improvement initiative required for accreditation, for instance), the rule does not define this as marketing or, therefore, as requiring authorization, even though PHI—including clinical information—was used to create the mailing list.

 A Marketer's Guide to HIPAA: Resources for Creating Effective and Compliant Marketing

Scenario: The poll

Q A facility is planning an expansion and wants input from its patients. The marketing department sends a questionnaire to all active patients, asking their opinion on various building and service options. The poll is intended to gauge how likely patients are to use different services in different locations, so that the CE can implement those most likely to generate the highest volume of visits. Is this an acceptable use of PHI without authorization?

A Yes. Whether it falls under the marketing exclusion for communications about services, or under healthcare operations rather than marketing, the CE's use of PHI in this case appears to meet Privacy Rule requirements.

Fundraising

In some healthcare organizations the marketing and fundraising functions are closely connected or even merged. Both functions have a public relations aspect, and a successful marketing campaign is likely to enhance fundraising initiatives.

HIPAA's Privacy Rule permits CEs to use certain PHI for raising funds for its own benefit without requiring authorization. However, there are three conditions.

1. The PHI that may be used is limited to the following:

   • Demographic information relating to an individual
   • Dates of healthcare provided to an individual.

2. The rule requires that CEs state clearly in their privacy notices that they intends to use such PHI for fundraising.

3. All fundraising materials sent to patients or plan members must describe how the recipient can opt out of receiving further fundraising communications. And the CE must make reasonable efforts to ensure that people who opt out are not sent fundraising communications in the future.

Also note that an institutionally related foundation to the CE may also

 A Marketer's Guide to HIPAA: Resources for Creating Effective and Compliant Marketing

use certain PHI for fundraising for the CE. A CE is also permitted to disclose the PHI specified above to a BA to assist with fundraising tasks.

Keep in mind that only the PHI listed above may be used without authorization. If any other PHI is used—for example, identifying cancer patients to target for raising funds for a new cancer center—then the conditions described here are no longer met and authorization is required.

Of course, if no PHI is used for fundraising—for instance, if only purchased lists are used—then those fundraising activities are outside the scope of HIPAA. However, it is still prudent to include opt-out instructions as a good public-relations practice.

Using PHI in ways that require authorization

Most communications defined as marketing by HIPAA require prior authorization. Any time a CE intends to disclose PHI to a third party for that party's (or another party's) marketing purposes, the CE must first obtain authorization.

Note that every mention of "authorization" in this book refers to the type of authorization epitomized by the form that is explained in Chapter 5. The Privacy Rule contains very explicit and detailed requirements that must be followed for authorization to be considered valid. **Generic, or blanket, authorizations are not valid for these purposes.**

Some communications between a CE and its patients or plan members that (one) might assume to be marketing are not. Be sure to read Chapter 4 to learn which communications HIPAA excludes from its definition of marketing. Once again, HIPAA generally considers marketing to be certain communications from a CE to its patients or plan members that encourage the individuals to use or purchase a product or service. Specifically, a CE must obtain authorizations when a CE offers value-added services and items (VAIS) to its patients or members and those VAIS are not health-related, or when the offers are available to the public and not exclusive to the CE.

Scenario: Maternity ward photographer

Q When admitting women about to give birth, a hospital asks each patient to sign an authorization form permitting the hospital to give a professional photographer her name and room number so the photographer can visit while she's in the hospital. The hospital gives a local photographer a daily list with the names and room numbers of women who have just given birth and who have signed this authorization form. The photographer then visits each of these patients to ask if she is interested in ordering a baby photo package. Is the hospital required to obtain authorization?

A Yes. Because the hospital is disclosing PHI to a third party (the photographer) for the third party's marketing opportunity, the hospital must first obtain an explicit authorization from each affected patient.

Scenario: New parenthood services

Q A health plan identifies new parents and requests that they sign an authorization permitting the plan to offer them a variety of discounts related to parenthood. Those who sign the authorization form are mailed a letter congratulating them on becoming parents, coupons for diaper services and local take-out restaurants, and a parenting magazine subscription. Must the health plan get authorization for this service?

A Yes. Because the health plan is offering nonhealth-related products and services, and the discounts are not unique to this plan, the plan must first obtain authorizations from the targeted members.

Scenario: Survey and drug sample

Q A hospital identifies patients with a certain diagnosis and mails them a letter describing a new drug on the market. The letter further explains that the pharmaceutical company that developed the drug would like to contact the patients, but only patients who sign their authorization form. When the signed forms are returned, the hospital compiles a list of those patients and their contact information for the drug company's BA, as instructed. The BA then mails those patients a survey and a free drug sample on behalf of the drug company. Is authorization necessary for this marketing effort?

A Yes. Although the hospital's providers are permitted to communicate with their patients about alternative medications and to hand out samples in the doctor's office without any authorization, this scenario involves the hospital releasing its PHI to a third party for another party's own marketing. Therefore, the hospital must send out authorization forms and only release PHI for patients who sign the form.

Scenario: Hospital mailing about new cardiac facility

Q A hospital sends a mailing to its patients, telling them about a cardiac facility, not part of the hospital, that can provide a baseline EKG for $39. Is this a violation of HIPAA?

A Yes. This communication is marketing, as defined by HIPAA, because the communication is not for the purpose of providing treatment advice. Hence, it should not have been sent without first obtaining authorization from its intended recipients.

HIPAA marketing question from the field

Q We are a community health center that is funded by HHS' Bureau of Primary Health Care, a state agency, and the United Way. The United Way has asked to photograph clients for brochures, newsletters, and its Web site. We've used a release form in the past, but is this sufficient? Are photos taken for fundraising considered PHI?

A First, some healthcare programs funded by federal grants are outside the scope of HIPAA's Administrative Simplification rules. Following the Privacy Rule may be good practice in such organizations, but it is not required. Be sure you understand what makes a provider a covered entity (CE)—that is, whether or not Administrative Simplification applies to your organization.

As to the release of photos, photographs are considered protected health information (PHI) in the context of a CE. And this example falls outside of disclosure for treatment, payment, or healthcare operations, public health, national priorities, etc. Thus, it requires that the CE obtain a HIPAA-compliant authorization, signed by the patient (or patient's representative), prior to release of photos or release of patient contact information if the United Way wishes to contact patients and ask to photograph them. These authorizations must carry an end date or end event. And keep in mind that authorizations are revocable, so be prepared to implement procedures for notifying the United Way if a patient revokes authorization.

Source: **Briefings on HIPAA,** *published by HCPro, Inc. August 2003*

Testimonials and referrals

There are other common practices for using patient information in ways that are viewed as marketing but do not fall within the marketing definition in HIPAA's Privacy Rule. The Privacy Rule writers viewed marketing as using PHI to target specific patients. However, there are examples of marketing initiatives using PHI to promote the organization to others.

Although these cases fall outside HIPAA's marketing definition, the Privacy Rule makes clear that CEs may not use PHI for purposes other than treatment, payment, or healthcare operations (TPO) without first getting an explicit authorization from the patient.

For example, a patient must sign an authorization form before a CE may display or publicize a patient's testimonial. In the case of testimonials, the

---

Scenario: Using patient testimonials

Q A hospital's marketing department collects testimonial letters and photographs from satisfied patients and displays them in the hospital's waiting rooms. This same hospital also includes patient testimonials in its advertising campaigns. The marketing director was careful to work with the privacy officer and obtain patient authorizations clearly stating how patients' PHI would be used. Is this scenario appropriate under HIPAA?

A Yes. The marketing director is taking steps to ensure the hospital's compliance with the Privacy Rule by first obtaining each patient's informed permission via an authorization form.

Scenario: Thanking a patient for a referral

Q Janet is very happy with the outcome of her elective cosmetic surgery. She tells her friend Kayla about the experience and suggests that Kayla call Dr. Bob Brown at the surgery center to make an appointment. Kayla calls and later sees Dr. Brown. Dr. Brown dictates a letter to Janet, thanking her for sending Kayla to him. Is this acceptable under HIPAA?

A No. It may be standard practice to send referral thank-you letters from one provider to another, and this is generally acceptable as patient treatment and continuity of care. But it is not appropriate to send a similar thank-you letter to a patient or other non-provider, because this is an improper disclosure of PHI. That is, the letter lets the recipient know that the person referred has become a patient. And the disclosure is not for TPO. In this scenario, it's up to Kayla to let Janet know that she's seen Dr. Brown, or to keep it a secret, if she chooses.

Dr. Brown has several HIPAA-compliant options, however. He could ask Kayla to sign an authorization letting him thank Janet for the referral. Or, he could periodically include in a newsletter or other notice a general thank-you to all patients or community residents who have referred people to him and to the surgery center.

Another HIPAA marketing question from the field

Q What does HIPAA say about physicians posting a sign in the waiting room thanking certain patients for referring others to the practice or posting a picture and name of a patient of the month?

A HIPAA's Privacy Rule allows for inadvertent disclosures, but only if you assessed the risk and took appropriate measures to limit such disclosures. For example, patients will see each other in a waiting room or semiprivate hospital room, and that can't be helped.

However, the sorts of disclosures in this question don't fall into that category. Keep in mind that use and disclosure of PHI for the purposes of treatment, payment, and the entity's healthcare operations are permitted. But most other uses and disclosures require the patient's explicit authorization.

Although the intent is to demonstrate appreciation for patients, waiting room postings appear to be an inappropriate disclosure of PHI unless the doctor has first let each named patient know how the practice intends to use his or her PHI. The doctor must obtain specific authorization to use the PHI in that manner, permitting refusal without retaliation.

Source: **Briefings on HIPAA,** *published by HCPro, Inc., May 2006*

patient is not the target of the marketing, but the CE is using and disclosing PHI to enhance its marketing—not for TPO.

Drawbacks

There are some clear disincentives for CEs engaging in marketing activities that require authorization.

First, there is administrative overhead in preparing and collecting valid, signed authorization forms. A portion of patients or plan members will not sign the authorization. And, because authorizations must be time- or event-limited and for a specific purpose (blanket authorizations are defective), all uses or disclosures of PHI in such cases must be carefully monitored for compliance.

If a CE intends to disclose its PHI for a third party's marketing purposes, the CE can only release the PHI of those individuals who sign an authorization. Given today's public concern for privacy, that number may be limited.

Given all these factors, CEs should analyze the types of specialties and issues that need to be marketed to the audience. CEs must determine whether it's worth investing resources in a campaign that will require authorizations. After all, they may be able to get the point/sale across by circumnavigating HIPAA. But there will be times—in order to have an effective campaign— when they'll have to go through the hassle of working through the authorization process. After such an analysis, many CEs may conclude that using PHI for marketing that requires authorization is a less viable option than (a) using PHI in ways that do not require authorization or (b) not using PHI at all.

Use of preexisting databases with PHI

Note that CEs are not permitted to use PHI from databases populated prior to the Privacy Rule enforcement date for marketing purposes unless the CE has first obtained authorizations. These databases are not "grandfathered" or exempted from the rule. HHS gave CEs two years to come into rule compliance and to obtain authorizations. Also note that blanket authorizations for marketing are not valid.

Of course, information used for communications that do not meet the HIPAA definition of marketing or are exceptions may not require individual authorization. For example, a hospital may use PHI in a pre existing database to mail newsletters with general health and wellness information.

7

Marketing and public relations options that avoid HIPAA

7

Marketing and public relations options that avoid HIPAA

Many healthcare organizations successfully carry out marketing and public relations activities without using their internal patient or plan member databases, thus avoiding any potential for a conflict with HIPAA regulations.

Marketing without a database

Traditional marketing is often conducted through mass media. This approach can be taken to more effective levels when focused on highly targeted media, such as marketing in specialized print publications, radio formats, cable TV, and other media. For example, a healthcare organization that wants to target older demographics may choose to advertise on an "oldies"-formatted radio station or place ads or inserts in a senior citizen publication. Obviously, this not as targeted as a direct message using a database, but it is an acceptable alternative if the media buy has been carefully researched.

Take a marketing "walk-through"

Your current patients are a captive audience, ready to listen to your message. The successful healthcare practice will look at the entire patient experience as a huge marketing opportunity. The best approach to using the patient experience as a marketing tool is to actually do a "walk-through" as a patient. Where in the patient flow would individuals be receptive to your marketing? Where are there opportunities for improved customer service that will make patients want to come back the next time they need treatment?

Waiting areas and exam rooms are the best sites for a receptive audience. If patients are not interested in the available magazines, they may thumb through attractive brochures describing your organization's services, or copies of past newsletters. This approach also provides an opportunity to reach family members or other visitors who may be accompanying patients. Every exam room should have posters and literature for patients to look at while waiting to be seen. An advanced practice may even choose to play videos or "infomercials" about procedures and educational topics. This should be done carefully, so that people are not forced to watch the video, but may choose to go to a separate area where the video is playing.

Involve staff

Your staff should not only be providing care, but each one should be a salesperson for your facility. To promote a new program or procedure through employees, have staff wear buttons that say "Ask me about . . ." Create incentive programs to encourage direct staff participation in marketing efforts. For example, when a parent brings a child's prescription into a pharmacy, the pharmacist may suggest adding cherry flavoring for an additional charge to make the medication easier to administer to the child. For every 10 "flavor upgrades," the pharmacist gets a gift card or other incentive reward.

Take advantage of on-hold messaging

On hold-messaging is a way to reach another captive audience. People who call your organization may be current patients or plan members, or they may be potential customers who have already selected your organization to contact. If a caller is placed on hold, it's a chance for them to hear messages offering information on your new or improved products or services. On-hold messages should consist of a loop of about 10 messages that are 15–20 seconds in length, alternating with similar-length periods of pleasant music.

Harness the power of your Web site

Your organization's Web site is an important marketing tool. If someone is visiting your Web site, it's likely that he or she is already an interested prospect, whom you need to convert into a customer. Your Web site's appearance, content, and ease of use can work favorably to keep current customers and attract new patients or plan members. Offer to mail or e-mail your newsletter to anyone who provides his or her name and mailing/e-mail address.

Distributing ad specialties and giveaways with your organization's name and logo, or promoting a new service or product, are other common marketing tactics, as described in the previous chapter, and are permitted by HIPAA.

These are just a few of the hundreds (if not thousands) of ideas that can be used to convey a marketing message to people who are probably in your protected health information (PHI) database without actually using that database and, therefore, bypassing the related HIPAA concerns. These mass media and internal marketing methods should be tracked for return on investment (ROI) purposes. A healthcare organization should review its marketing plan monthly or quarterly to assess success in marketing activities and adjust them, if necessary.

Database marketing

While traditional mass-marketing methods are often successful, nothing can replicate the power of delivering a specific message to a specific (i.e., defined) individual. This can be done without tapping into your internal PHI databases. Purchasing lists of individuals is a long-standing marketing practice. Lists can be based on demographics, such as women over 50; on geographic information, such as addresses within a cluster of ZIP Codes; and on psychosocial data, such as income, spending patterns, and other personal habits. These purchased lists may actually be more successful than your internal patient lists for database marketing, because they include people who are not already your patients or customers. This infuses "new blood" into your potential market.

Scenario: Marketing to a third-party list

Q A hospital has recently opened a new obstetrics practice. The marketing department buys a list of women ages 18–40 living in the hospital's geographic area and mails a general letter to everyone on the list, telling them about the new service. A marketing department employee comments that some of these women must already be patients at the hospital. Because some of the letter recipients are also patients, is this letter a violation of HIPAA?

A No. Because the marketing list was purchased from a third party and not derived from the hospital's patient database, the letter is acceptable under HIPAA. Any overlap with patients is coincidental.

Creating valuable lists without using PHI

Covered entities (CEs) can also create their own lists, as long as they steer clear of PHI. For example, a CE (or a business associate [BA] working on behalf of a CE) may solicit information through a survey at a local mall. People choosing to participate would voluntarily provide personally identifiable information, such as name and address. Participants may be asked their opinions of a planned new facility or service and whether they are likely to use it, how often they seek treatment, or whether they would be likely to change health plans under various conditions. This type of information can be useful to an organization, yet is not under the limitations of HIPAA.

Another option for building a non-PHI database is through a personal opt-in mailing request. Place signup cards in the waiting room or other area for patients and visitors to fill out to be placed on your mailing list to receive newsletters and other general information. You may have seen this type of intake card in retail stores, where customers request to be placed on the mailing list for catalogs or other sales promotion materials. Just remember when designing these intake cards not to solicit health-related information that could be considered PHI. And although this is outside the scope of HIPAA, be sure to include instructions for being removed from the mailing list.

You can also work through nonprofit groups to get your message to a list of targeted people. For example: You could work with the local diabetes support group by providing postage and a preprinted insert about your excellent diabetes program to include in their monthly newsletter. If you're trying to reach diabetics, this is a great way to mail a piece that will actually be read by a targeted group, while at the same time promoting community relations. It's a win-win situation for both entities. The support group finds a way to save money on mailing costs, and you find a way to reach a wider audience than you could have reached with your own PHI database of current patients.

Strategies for ensuring compliance

Strategies for ensuring compliance

Compliance begins with education. Management and staff need to be aware of the details within HIPAA's Privacy Rule that apply to marketing and the use of protected patient data. Here is a quick summary of HIPAA's Privacy Rule position on covered entities (CEs) using or disclosing protected health information (PHI) for marketing purposes:

a. No authorization needed: As a CE, most communications you are likely to have with your patients and plan members are permitted by HIPAA without taking any special steps. Typically, health and treatment communications, as well as communications about your health-related products and services, are not considered marketing by the Privacy Rule, even if they also promote or provide a clear benefit to your organization.

b. Always get authorization: At the other end of the spectrum, disclosing (releasing) your patients' or plan members' PHI to a third party for that or some other party's marketing purposes always requires prior authorization. And some marketing activities overlooked by HIPAA—such as using patients' testimonial and photographs in marketing materials—always require authorization. Whenever authorization is required, be sure to follow all the specifications to ensure your authorizations are valid.

   c. It depends: In between the two types of activities above, there is a fuzzy area—such as when a CE uses its PHI to market a third party's product to its patients or plan members—where CEs first must carefully consider what they plan to do and whether or not it requires authorization.

In the following section, we'll discuss tips for staying on top of HIPAA privacy recommendations that will keep your organization in compliance and out of hot water.

Be well grounded in applicable laws and regulations

Marketing departments exist to enhance the organization and contribute to revenue, directly and indirectly. At the same time, marketing initiatives must meet legal requirements and constraints.

Be aware of all laws and regulations—international, federal, state, and local—relating to patient or plan member (customer) privacy and marketing that govern your organization. Stay on top of this information by communicating with legal counsel, joining regional and industry collaboratives, and checking the Internet. Become familiar with the principles of personal information privacy so that you can ensure compliance with the full intent of relevant laws and regulations.

In addition to HIPAA, there are federal and state do-not-call and do-not-mail lists, as well as opting out of electronic marketing through the CAN-SPAM law. Understand how and when to use these lists to exclude people who do not want to receive marketing. Make it simple for people who receive your marketing materials to opt out of future communications. Develop your own do-not-contact list. Directing communications to these people will only result in possible complaints (including a HIPAA complaint that carries civil penalties) and wasted resources.

Educate staff

CEs are required to provide privacy and security training to the full workforce, including staff responsible for marketing. If you are fortunate enough to have a marketing staff, be sure their HIPAA training goes beyond the standard content geared toward the general workforce. Clinical and administrative staff typically do not need to understand the HIPAA details related to marketing, but the marketing team must have a solid grasp of the topic.

Use the following strategies to ensure staff compliance:

Raise the topic frequently: Plan to bring up the topic of HIPAA privacy and security to your staff on a regular and frequent basis, such as monthly. This keeps the topic in mind, and it sends a message that management believes it's important.

Focus on sound bites: Don't try to cover everything at once. When you bring up privacy and security, focus on one discrete point. Use a recent work incident or a news article to generate discussion, for example.

Incorporate resources: Use, and refer curious staff to, resources such as this book and others, the U.S. Health and Human Services Web site, and other Internet resources listed in the Resources section of this book to learn more about HIPAA, privacy, and information security.

"Sell" your training: Consider becoming a key player in your organization's HIPAA-mandated privacy and security training, and bring your marketing skills to the table. Privacy and security programs need to be sold to the workforce, and this can be done through well-crafted training materials. Look for posters to display. Run a contest to select the best program name and mascot/slogan (such as "Loose lips sink ships"). Purchase or develop

Quick training solutions for busy managers

Consider using one or more of these methods to educate staff about HIPAA privacy and security issues at your organization:

Posters. Posters are an underrated method of reminding staff about key training points. They are simple to create and can be effective if they're hung where people will see them often. A quick glance could mean the difference between a staff member remembering or forgetting small details about the Privacy Rule.

Paycheck stuffers. A card in the envelope with staff members' paychecks is a very effective way of communicating rule updates or reinforcing policy or procedure changes. You know they will get the message, and that's half the battle.

Company newsletters. Articles in your company's employee newsletter that focus on news stories in relation to your organization's privacy and security policies can be a great way to present your entire staff with scenarios. These articles might answer questions that staff members may have about HIPAA, privacy, and security but are reluctant to ask a supervisor or privacy officer. I think it's unlikely that the full workforce ever gets involved in marketing questions. I don't recommend this broad training in marketing, especially because the scenarios usually turn on very narrow points. Better to get the full workforce on board with what they really need to know.

Training packets. Self-learning packets or online modules are especially effective if you're dealing with staff who are constantly on the go. The content can summarize your training topics and allow your staff to get the training they need without trying to rearrange their schedules to accommodate training sessions. Consider giving them a three-ring binder so they can store these packets in one place and refer back to them when they need them.

products such as PowerPoint presentations and weekly e-mail reminders, which will keep staff informed of evolving healthcare legislation like HIPAA.

Work with your privacy officer

Develop a good working relationship with your organization's privacy officer (PO). You are likely to know as much or more about HIPAA's stance on marketing as the PO does, so the alliance is one of mutual benefit.

Be sure to communicate with your PO whenever you are considering engaging a third party. That third-party vendor may or may not become a HIPAA-defined business associate (BA). But if it does, the PO (or designee) will need to add the business name and contact information to your organization's list of its BAs, and he or she will also need to prepare a BA contract. To protect your organization and your PHI, the BA contract, or an overarching contract to which it is an addendum, should specify the marketing tasks you are hiring the company to perform. Remember that no PHI may be released to a BA until the contract is signed. (See Appendix B for details about the content of BA contracts.)

Further, businesses such as mail houses and telemarketing firms may not be very familiar with HIPAA requirements, and BAs are responsible for ensuring privacy and security of PHI. Take the extra step to assess how HIPAA-savvy your BA is. If you have any concern that a BA is not fully aware of its role in terms of HIPAA, or that a BA is not taking it seriously, you have an obligation to address the problem. Start by bringing it to the attention of your PO, and then work with the PO to develop a course of action.

Remember that there can be serious consequences for the CE if the BA causes an avoidable breach of HIPAA requirements.

Monitor marketing activities

Be sure that all marketing initiatives using databases or PHI are routinely subject to a documented review to ensure that they meet HIPAA and other legal requirements. Set up a simple review process and documentation format. Train staff in how to carry out the procedure, and then periodically verify that the process is being followed. It is particularly valuable to have a documented process in a midsize or large department, where new marketing projects or modifications to a marketing strategy might be made without clear oversight.

Your monitoring process should be a three-step effort:

1. Plan and document a review procedure and form. The procedure should define when the form should be completed, by whom, where it should be filed and how, etc.

2. Train staff in how to carry out the procedure. Assign responsibilities.

3. Periodically verify that the process is being followed. This, too, should be a documented process, with assigned responsibility and details of how to carry it out. For example, verification might include a step to select a

random subset of patients from the marketing list or database, and then pull their signed authorization forms.

Developing a review form

As you develop the review form, you may want to include items such as the following:

- Brief description or project name of the marketing initiative.

- Start date and projected end date/event (or "open").

- Indication as to whether PHI will be used. For example, "Will the project use patient (or plan member) information—that is, PHI? If yes, does the project require patient (or plan member) authorization (either because it is defined as marketing or because it is outside permissible uses/disclosures of PHI)?"

If the answer to the above is "yes," then consider adding the following:

- Describe what patient (or plan member) data elements will be used, and how

- Attach a copy of the authorization form prepared for this project

- Attach a description of how authorizations are obtained for this project (e.g., explanatory cover letter mailed to individuals)

- Attach a brief description of how you will ensure that only individuals who have signed authorizations will be used in this marketing project and how you will ensure that their PHI will not be used other than as authorized

While the emphasis here is on HIPAA, also include checks to ensure compliance with other relevant laws and regulations.

It's a good idea to involve your PO in these monitoring efforts, for a number of reasons. First, you are likely to gain his or her respect and appreciation for taking this responsibility. Second, your PO may choose to participate in developing these procedures and documentation, or at least review them before they are implemented. Last, your PO may be the person who performs the periodic review or oversight of marketing project regulatory compliance.

Handling HIPAA complaints effectively

If the marketing department receives complaints that the CE is violating HIPAA or other privacy regulations through its marketing activities, be sure to refer them immediately to your PO (and legal counsel, depending on your organization). Because HIPAA requires CEs to have a formal complaint-handling process, your organization is likely to have a form on which to submit privacy/security complaints. It should also have procedures in place for investigating and responding to complaints. Be cooperative and stay in close communication to the PO as he or she coordinates and resolves the issue.

The future of privacy

Now that you better understand how to market your organization in the new world of HIPAA's Privacy Rule, remember that this is a starting point, not an end point.

HIPAA's final Privacy Rule is anything but final. It's true that the first iteration of a set of national health privacy standards is now enforceable, but this marks only the beginning of a new stage in the policy debate about the "right" balance between personal privacy protections and the expedient use of electronic health records.

HHS reserves the right to change the rules annually, and we should expect that the government will do so. Privacy Rule changes may be minor adjustments or significant rewrites, and may be due to industry pressure, change in administration (i.e., a newly elected president in 2008), and major events such as another "9/11" terrorist attack. HIPAA's security standards, on the other hand, are industry-neutral and are likely to move in one direction: toward stronger controls.

Given the uncertainty of the regulatory future, it seems prudent from both a business perspective and an ethical standpoint for healthcare organizations to strive for good privacy principles and practices, regardless of the details of current regulations. Whatever the shift in details, an organization's strong privacy culture prepares it to easily address new requirements and, more important, assure that our personal health information is always treated with care.

Glossary

Glossary

Common HIPAA terms

Authorization—An authorization with a specific purpose (e.g., at the patient's request, patient authorizes hospital to release record to a named third party; or at the hospital's request, patient authorizes hospital to use or disclose information for a specified "unusual" purpose, such as marketing). It is almost always voluntary on the part of the patient, and the covered entity may not withhold treatment or payment if the patient refuses to sign. It is revocable, and it must have an expiration date or event.

Business associate (BA)—Third parties that assist a CE in performing its work involving PHI. For example, many providers use external transcription, coding, billing, and collections companies. And many CEs use accreditation agencies, legal firms, and software vendors that, in some cases, have access to PHI. Because HHS does not have regulatory authority over these types of businesses, the rules hold CEs accountable, to some extent, for

BAs' actions regarding protection of PHI. Note that in some instances the BA is also a CE, in which case the BA is directly responsible for HIPAA compliance.

Covered entity (CE)—An individual or organization that is subject to the rules. CEs include all health plans, from traditional insurers, such as Blue Cross Blue Shield, to government programs, such as Medicare and Medicaid. CEs are also healthcare clearinghouses that often reformat and retransmit transactions for these entities. And finally, CEs are healthcare providers that engage in electronic transmission of any of these transactions. (Note that providers who are strictly paper-based or do not interact with insurance plans are not covered by Administrative Simplification.)

Designated record set (DRS)—A group of records maintained by or for a CE and used by the CE to make decisions about individuals. This broad record set includes providers' medical and billing records, as well as health plans' enrollment, payment, claims adjudication, and case management records. It also includes information received from other sources. In the case of a provider, information from other sources includes records received from another treatment provider. A DRS may be in either paper or electronic form.

Disclosure—The release of, transfer of, provision of access to, or divulging in any manner of information outside the entity holding the information. (Compare to "Use.")

Healthcare—Care, services, or supplies related to the health of an individual. Healthcare includes, but is not limited to, the following:

- Preventive, diagnostic, therapeutic, rehabilitative, maintenance, or palliative care, and counseling, service, assessment, or procedure with respect to the physical or mental condition, or functional status, of an individual or that affects the structure or function of the body; and

- Sale or dispensing of a drug, device, equipment, or other item in accordance with a prescription.

Healthcare operations—The following activities of the CE to the extent that the activities are related to covered functions . . .

(1) Conducting quality assessment and improvement activities . . .

(2) Reviewing the competence or qualifications of healthcare professionals, . . . conducting training programs . . . , accreditation, certification, licensing, or credentialing activities

(3) Underwriting, premium rating, and other activities relating to the creation, renewal, or replacement of a contract of health insurance . . . for reinsurance . . . including stop-loss and excess of loss insurance . . . [with some conditions]

(4) Conducting or arranging for medical review, legal services, and auditing functions, including fraud and abuse detection and compliance programs;

(5) Business planning and development, such as conducting cost-management and planning-related analyses . . .

(6) Business management and general administrative activities, including . . . customer service, . . . resolution of internal grievances; . . . due diligence in connection with the sale or transfer of assets, . . . creating de-identified health information . . .

Notice of privacy practices—This notice must include the header, "THIS NOTICE DESCRIBES HOW MEDICAL INFORMATION ABOUT YOU MAY BE USED AND DISCLOSED AND HOW YOU CAN GET ACCESS TO THIS INFORMATION. PLEASE REVIEW IT CAREFULLY." The notice describes all the legally required and permitted uses and disclosures of personal health data by that CE, as well as the individual's privacy rights and how to exercise them. There are specific requirements for the content and for how the notice must be provided to patients and plan members (which differs for providers and plans).

Payment—Activities undertaken by

(i) a health plan to obtain premiums or to determine or fulfill its responsibility for coverage and provision of benefits under the health plan; or

(ii) a covered healthcare provider or health plan to obtain or provide reimbursement for the provision of health care;

and for the purpose of

(i) determination of eligibility

(ii) risk adjusting

(iii) billing, claims management, collections, payment for reinsurance

(iv) review for medical necessity

(v) utilization review

(vi) certain disclosures to consumer reporting agencies

Personal representative—A person who has the authority to act on behalf of an individual in making decisions related to healthcare, such as giving authorization for use of PHI. This may be next-of-kin, a person with healthcare power of attorney, or the executor or administrator of a deceased patient's estate. Be sure also to see state laws and seek legal counsel when in doubt.

Protected health information (PHI)—The information that CEs are required to protect and keep confidential through their privacy and security programs as specified in those rules. Essentially, it is any information that could reasonably be used to identify a given patient or plan member. PHI can appear in any form, including oral, paper, and electronic interactions.

Be aware that PHI goes beyond direct identifiers such as name, medical record number, and plan member ID, and may include indirect information that—when coupled with other information, such as publicly available census data—could be used to identify an individual. In some cases, even a diagnosis code or an occupation descriptor can be enough information to reveal a person's identity. Note that PHI includes—and does not distinguish between—demographic, financial, and clinical data about a patient or plan member.

Summary health information—Information that may be individually identifiable (most HIPAA-defined identifiers must be deleted, but with some exceptions), and that summarizes claims history, expenses, or type of claims experienced by individuals for whom a plan sponsor has provided health benefits under a group health plan. This information may be disclosed to plan sponsors for the limited purposes of (a) obtaining premium bids from health plans for providing coverage under the group health plan, or (b) modifying, amending, or terminating the group health plan. If more PHI is disclosed or if it is used for other than the above purposes, then the plan documents must be amended as specified in the Privacy Rule, and a certificate (certifying that the plan documents have been so amended) presented to the insurer or third party administrator disclosing the PHI to the plan sponsor.

Treatment—The provision, coordination, or management of healthcare and related services by one or more healthcare providers, . . . including . . . coordination by a healthcare provider with a third party; consultation between healthcare providers relating to a patient; or the referral of a patient for healthcare from one healthcare provider to another.

Treatment, payment, or healthcare operations (TPO)—Commonly abbreviated as TPO, these three functions are treated similarly under most HIPAA privacy provisions.

Use—Sharing employment, application, utilization, examination, or analysis of individually identifiable health information *within* an entity that maintains such information. (Compare to "Disclosure.")

Workforce—A term used in the rules to include a CE's employees, as well as its unpaid volunteers, students, and even individuals who may be involved in the CE's training program. In short, workforce refers to any individuals working under the control of the CE, whether they're being paid or not. The rules clearly hold CEs responsible for training, compliance, and sanctions for their workforce. (Note that workforce members and business associates are mutually exclusive categories.)

Note: Please note that these may be abbreviated, abridged, and/or paraphrased versions of what is contained in the HIPAA Rules. Italics have been added for emphasis. For the exact language in the Privacy Rule, please refer to the Dec. 28, 2000 Federal Register. For further explanation, read the preamble in the Federal Register and the Privacy Rule update published in the Federal Register on Aug. 14, 2002.

Resources

Resources

Health information security and privacy

1. Government regulations

   HIPAA Administrative Simplification *[www.cms.hhs.gov/HIPAAGenInfo/]*

   HHS Office for Civil Rights *[www.hhs.gov/ocr]* (administers HIPAA Privacy Rule)

   Federal legislation *[thomas.loc.gov]*

   State legislation *[www.ncsl.org]*

2. Organizations

   Health Privacy Project *[www.healthprivacy.org]*

   AHIMA *[www.ahima.org]*

Massachusetts Health Data Consortium *[www.mahealthdata.org]*

North Carolina Healthcare Info & Communications Alliance *[www.nchica.org]*

California HealthCare Foundation *[www.chcf.org]*

3. Training and products
HCPro *[www.hcpro.com]* (newsletters, audioconferences, training materials, books)

MIS Training Institute *[www.misti.com]* (HealthSec annual conference, seminars)

Marketing

Direct Marketing Association (DMA) *[www.the-dma.org]*

DMA's HIPAA FAQ *[www.the-dma.org/privacy/hipaafaqs.shtml]*

DMA's General Healthcare Marketing Cheatsheet *[www.the-dma.org/guidelines/healthdatafaqs.shtml]*

HHS Marketing Guidelines *[www.hhs.gov/ocr/hipaa/guidelines/marketing.pdf]*

Direct Magazine *[www.directmag.com]*

Society for Healthcare Strategy and Market Development (SHSMD) *[www.shsmd.org/shsmd/index.jsp]*

Public Relations Society of America's Health Academy *[www.healthacademy.prsa.org/]*

Information security (not specific to healthcare)

1. Security white papers, guidance
   NIST Computer Security Resource Center *[http://csrc.nist.gov]*
   SANS SCORE *[www.sans.org/score]* (technical best practices)

2. Education, training, and certification
   ISC *[www.isc2.org]* (CISSP certification)
   ISSA *[www.issa.org]* (professional association; meetings and newsletters)
   MIS Training Institute *[www.misti.com]* (conferences, seminars, work shops)
   SANS *[www.sans.org]* (conferences, seminars, workshops)

3. Security alerts (There are many more; see also your vendors, e.g., Microsoft)
   CERT *[www.cert.org]*
   CIAC *[www.ciac.org/ciac]*
   FIRST *[www.first.org]*

4. Publications

InfoSecurity News magazine (free) *[www.scmagazine.com/]*

Information Security magazine (free) *[informationsecurity.techtarget.com/]*

Auerbach Publications textbooks *[www.auerbach-publications.com]*

Appendix A:
HIPAA penalties

Appendix A:
HIPAA penalties

Civil penalty for failure to comply with Administrative Simplification requirements and standards

Offense	Fines
Failure to comply with a HIPAA provision	Up to $100 per person per violation Maximum of $25,000 per person for violation of a single standard in one calendar year

Criminal penalty for "wrongful disclosure of individually identifiable
health information"

Knowingly and in violation of HIPAA:

(1) using a unique health identifier OR

(2) obtaining identifiable health information OR

(3) disclosing identifiable health information

Offense	Fines and/or imprisonment
Knowing misuse	Up to $50,000 and/or up to one year's imprisonment
Knowing misuse under false pretenses	Up to $100,000 and/or up to five year's imprisonment
Knowing misuse with intent to sell, transfer, or use individually identifiable health information for commercial advantage, personal gain, or malicious harm	Up to $250,000 and/or up to 10 year's imprisonment

Appendix B: Requirements for business associate contracts

Appendix B: Requirements for business associate contracts

Both HIPAA's Privacy Rule and its Security Rule require covered entities (CEs) to have special legal agreements with their HIPAA-defined business associates (BAs) before any protected health information (PHI) may be released. The two rules are very similar on this topic and have the following requirements in common:

1. The BA contract (or other legal arrangement, such as a Memo of Understanding, in some circumstances) must meet specific content requirements of the two rules. (See below.)

2. The CE is deemed noncompliant if the CE knew of a pattern of activity or practice of the BA that is a material breach or violation of the BA contract, unless the CE took reasonable steps to cure the problem and, if those steps were unsuccessful,

- terminated the contract with the BA, or

- if termination was not feasible, notified the Secretary of HHS

3. If the BA is also a CE, the organization is directly subject to HIPAA penalties, even when acting in a BA capacity.

The implementation specifications for the BA contract in the two rules are similar and overlapping, but not identical.

As required by the Privacy Rule, the contract between a CE and BA must

- establish the permitted and required uses and disclosures of the CE's PHI by the BA

- provide that the BA will:

  - not further use or disclose the PHI except as permitted by the contract or required by law

  - use appropriate safeguards to prevent use or disclosure of the PHI other than as provided for by the contract

  - report to the CE any use or disclosure of the PHI not provided for by the contract, of which it becomes aware

- ensure that any agents to whom it provides the CE's PHI agree to the same restrictions and conditions that apply to the BA

- make the PHI available for various purposes, such as record amendment and HHS investigation

- at termination of the contract, if feasible, return or destroy all PHI; otherwise extend protections and limit further uses and disclosures of such PHI

- authorize termination of the contract by the CE if the CE determines that the BA has violated a material term of the contract

As required by the Security Rule, "The contract between a covered entity and a business associate must provide that the business associate will

- implement administrative, physical, and technical safeguards that reasonably and appropriately protect the confidentiality, integrity, and availability of the electronic protected health information that it creates, receives, maintains, or transmits on behalf of the covered entity as required by this subpart;

- ensure that any agent, including a subcontractor, to whom it provides such information agrees to implement reasonable and appropriate safeguards to protect it;

- report to the covered entity any security incident of which it becomes aware;

• authorize termination of the contract by the covered entity, if the covered entity determines that the business associate has violated a material term of the contract."

Suggestions

• Always have legal counsel review contracts. In this case, consider having legal counsel add language for indemnification and insurance coverage, and a change-of-law provision.

• Carefully describe what uses/disclosures of your PHI the BA is permitted to make.

• Document privacy and security incident reporting information, such as

- name and contact information for both the CE and the BA (typically the privacy and security officers at each organization)

- time frame(s) for reporting incidents to the CE (such as "within two business days")

Note: Please note that this information has been paraphrased based on what is contained in the HIPAA rules. Please consult the rules for full explanations.